THE INN OF THE BIRDS

The INN of the BIRDS

written and illustrated

by

ANTHONY RYE

FIRST PUBLISHED BY JONATHAN CAPE
REPRINTED BY THE SCOLAR PRESS
1970

FIRST PUBLISHED BY JONATHAN CAPE, 1947

To
EDMUND BLUNDEN

FIRST PRINTED BY THE ALDEN PRESS
REPRINTED IN GREAT BRITAIN BY
THE SCOLAR PRESS LTD., MENSTON, YORKS.
1970

CONTENTS

THE TABARD TREE

This is the Inn of the Birds;
This is the Tabard Tree;
Of green and puissant age,
Of ancient pilgrimage;
Into whose chambers infinite wings
Have folded narrowly.

Here comes that caravan
Of gypsy-flocking hordes
Bound in their sunward swings –
That die or change their Springs:
Who since their race began
Were shackled to a wheel,
And must obey the tyrannous air
Yet will a respite steal.

Of plumage gay and strange,
A host with various banners,
How willingly they exchange
Their perilous savannahs –
Their cold blind wastes and desolate air,
To flit and sing in sanctuary here!

A WARNING

These are our voices of joy and anger,
Passionate gladness, desperate alarm:
Our common speech in safety or in danger;
Ecstatic, never calm.

We have no words to pierce or soothe, slow stranger;
No cleaving tongues, no balm,
For your dull natures: though we meet you here,
It is to fly and spy and change our air.

But our bright wings, light bodies, eager stare,
Cut rapid syllables as if of fire
Into the silence; and could our desire
Be told more clearly? –
If you will, admire,
Or love us if you must . . . but not too nearly!

THE PARTRIDGE

Under the violet light that lies
In February after-skies,
Before the rains have washed them silver
That trickle down to dyke and culver,
The partridge on the plough-ridge creaks,
And new gloss on his feather sleeks.

ST. VALENTINE'S DAY

Valentine's Day is the birds' wedding day,
the old people say:

Then quickly come gliding
From Winter's dark hiding,
With short gleeful rushes,
The Blackbirds and Thrushes,
Robins and Finches,
And such feathered inches
As Titmice and Wrens.
Quite lost is the sense
Of the cold and despair
As they revel in flight
All a short day's delight;
Unthinking, unfearing,
At last disappearing
Pair by pair through the wintry air.

It is then the sun glows in the midst of the snows,
as every bird knows:

And as the warmth kindles,
Behold! the snow dwindles,
And phantoms of flowers
Appear in those hours
As if seen beneath ice
By a magic device.
The spectral sweet cherry
And fire-feigning berry
Come with ripening seeds
Then to cheapen all needs;
Each cockbird inspired,
To rivalry fired
By the year's flaunted colour,
Must sing out his valour,
While his hen pours her breast
In the cup of her nest,
As if it were May on St. Valentine's Day!

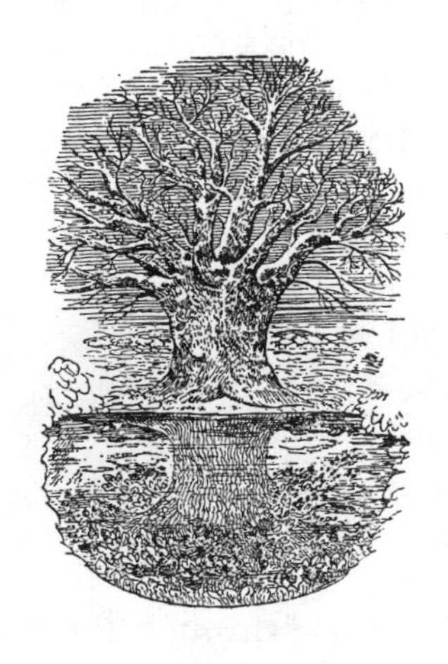

THE LAPWING

O Lapwing, stop your cries! –
Your sorrowful voice has wet my cheek:
For at the sound of it –
  'See-o-whit! See-o-whit!' –
My restless step grows weak.
I see the evening skies;
I smell the fresh-turned loam;
The same skies, the self-same fields,
  the very clods of home!

THE SPARROW HAWK

The blue hawk with the yellow eye
Passed close beside our hedge again:
What is it like to strike and gain?
What is it like to die?

The blackbird singing in the lane,
Suddenly he has ceased to sing:
Set to the blaze, and round it ring;
Shut out the sudden rain.

ROOKS AND DAWS

Primroses dotting the sheltered piece;
    The violet espied;
Ruffled water or smooth, that glints
    In pools on the grassy ride;
    Old elm trees in caprice,
    That toss their branches wide,
Flushing along their tops with the tints
Of the imminent gay Springtide:
    The green in filigree
    On the plinth of each ponderous tree;
And above all the call of the daws
And the rooks in the Jubilee:
Perilous, whipped by the wind like straws,
With black stiff sticks they fly,
Joyously battling with beak and claws
To their nests in the branches high.

CHIFF-CHAFF

Chiff-chaff, chiff-chaff,
After labour, rest I have;
After winter, sunny leisure;
After fever, water-pleasure:
Chiff-chaff, chiff-chaff . . .

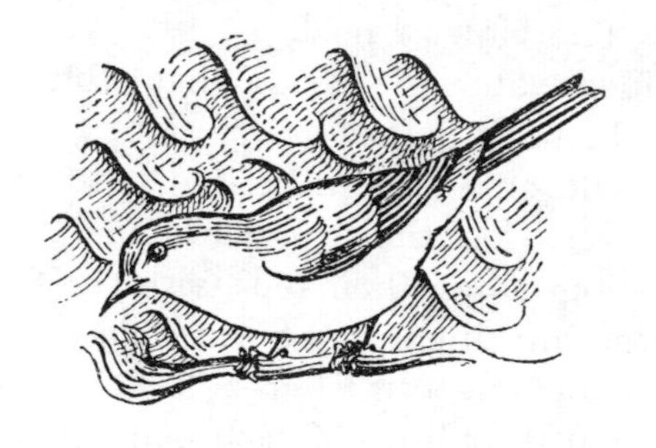

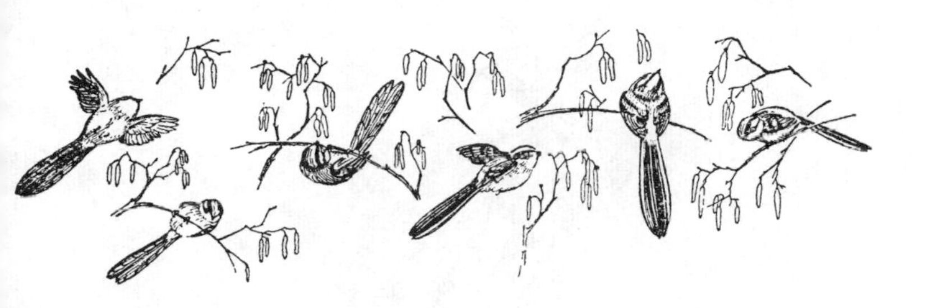

TITMICE

On a day when soft wet blue
The long smooth boughs seemed shining through,
A troop of birds on laughing wings
Came tumbling by in loops and strings:
  'See! See! See!' their leader cried,
And then they scattered far and wide.
Running and puzzling, up and down
The trees they blew, like thistledown.
Long after they had flown from me
I heard them shouting: 'See! See! See!'

GREEN WOODPECKER

O the merry bird – the gallant soldier!
He doubles on his drum
And wears a scarlet plume
Upon his head, and green upon his shoulder.

He doubles on his drum, the busy soldier,
As though he knew that Time and he grew older,
And leaps upon the air
As if he'd none to spare,
And feared the green already in the gold ear.

The woodman loves the bird, the merry soldier;
He smiles to hear that laughter growing bolder,
As through the wood it rings
To tell of happier Springs,
Joy of the new, derision on the old year.

THE CUCKOO

When the cuckoo's bell, dulcet and clear,
Rings to and fro in the morning air,
All the other birds are wakeful to hear,
And Summer comes and listens there.

MAGPIES

In a narrow plot of land,
Between hills, a fallow sodden,
Which man's indifferent hand
Seemed to have planted and forgotten –
A haggard, desolate place;
Where every bough was muted;
Where not a blackbird fluted,
Nor a missel-thrush even,
Whose songs by storm are driven
Out over wintry space:
From the shadow of a wood
Suddenly a merry rabble,
Magpies, a Summer brood,
Broke with melodious babble –
A blithe, tumultuous clack:
Perched on the rusty harrow,
Checkered the weedy fallow:
O blessed birds! white treason
You play on sense and season:
King Folly has come back!
Surely your saving voice is
Human of heavenly graces?
Laughter we cannot lack.

GOLDFINCHES

Goldfinches whistle, and fling
Through the air, and they cling
Upon thistles, and there
They find seeds, when like beads
Their eyes glisten:
O listen!

Who that has gold wants for money,
Or any
Fine clothes who has silk
Soft as milk,
Or the deepest of satin?
Or who would desire to be put in
A musty plush seat in the stalls
At a film, with the calls
Of these finches so bright
On his ears?
It appears
As a pattern
As tripping and brief as their flight
On the light
Breezes carried:
O hear it!

THE HERON

The heron plucks her dripping shanks
Out of the ooze, and bearing
Into the wind, with lavish sweep,
Mounts upward through the vapour-steep,
Steadily and unveering.

Shadow and bird a minute's space
Hang in the light together;
Then where the mass of the wood leans down,
Into the depth of its broad shade thrown,
Vanish, and none tells whither.

But in the height, high overhead,
We catch the slow vanes tilted;
The long legs jutting behind like spars,
And the beak like a dagger held at the stars;
All carried into the reddening west
While the mud still cloudily trails to rest,
Here where the tall bird stilted.

SWANS

Swans, for their beauty mute,
Have never one poor note:
But when they fly, the air between their wings
Rushes and sings.

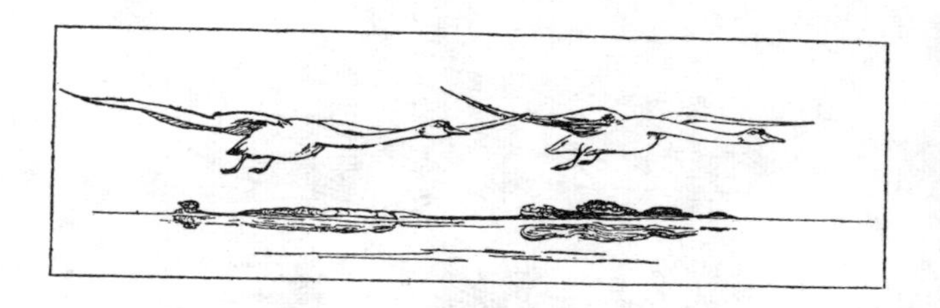

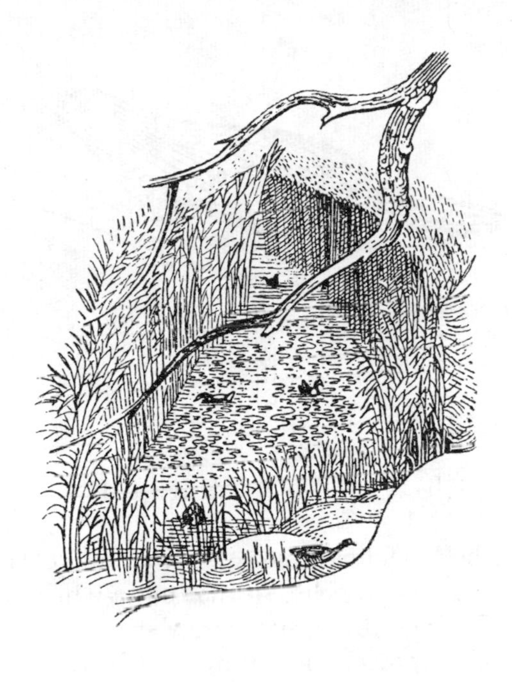

WATERBIRDS

Waterbirds calling, liquid and long;
Bright as the ripples, cold as the roots
They delve among.
At twilight, or early daylight,
In the still air,
Over the moulded, rosy or golden
Sand, which the tides lay bare:
Calling, calling a morning greeting,
And at nightfall repeating
The same freshness, the same beauty,
the same vision, cool and rare.

THE BLACKBIRD

The blackbird's note is round and clear,
And has an echo, so that everywhere
He sings there seems new space
Of Paradise, and young eyes looking out.

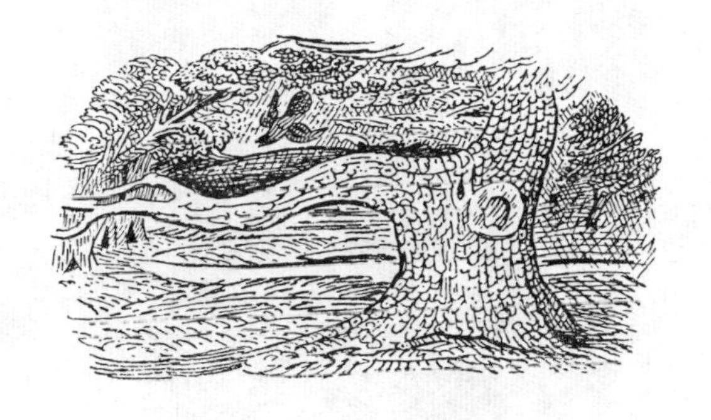

THE NIGHTJAR

The nightjar flicks his spinning wheels,
Then sits and sings like fishers' reels:
So is his love like their full creels.

THE KINGFISHER

His gladly singing plumes
The clear lake water glasses;
A shrill, sweet tune,
As over it he passes.

Of one phrase, long drawn out,
One chord of colours shaken
By an invisible bow all day,
To the eyes' vibration:
One chord of colour, deftly laid,
No echo making:
One phrase, – again! again!
So heard, so fading.

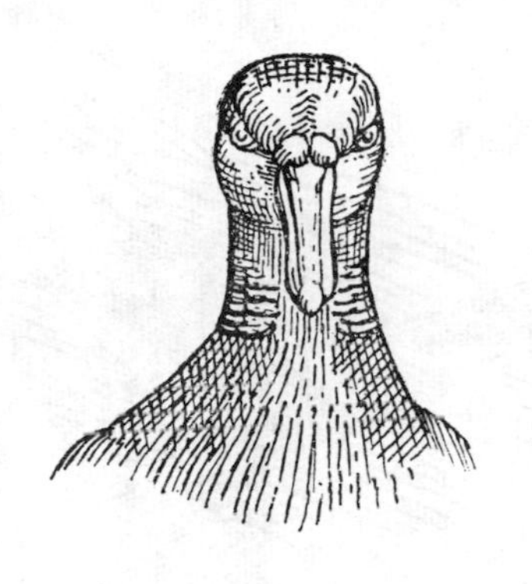

THE RING DOVE

For her rose and for her ring
Venus bids her bird to sing:
He, in modesty, puts on
The sober vestment of a nun.

THE WOOD WREN

Spin, coin of purest silver,
On platters of leaf gold;
Spin and ring, ring and spin,
Till the joy of it be told:
Ring it far and near,
Come, tell it in my ear;
Your little mite of maundy
As a charm I'll wear:
And the amplitude
Of my forest mood
Shall be sweetened as a bell
Is, into whose molten swell
A gift of silver fell.

THE CURLEW

The curlew's note comes fellowly
Over the wintry dune,
Though upon wings of fear she flies
The wraith of her own tune:

She threads her labyrinth of ways
While all aloft are driven,
Fledging the milky solitudes,
The white wind-flocks of heaven.

SPARROWS

Sparrows chirping, alert in the ivy leaves . . .
Almost no sound perhaps, of itself, at all;
But a stir of the air of the eaves,
An accompaniment to voices,
Like the shuffling of tired feet in the street,
Or the lapse of a coal in the grate.
Dullest of noises,
There in the dusty ivy against the wall;
The ivy, the thick ivy, which the wind has stirred,
Or their wings; which the rain has made bloom
Through the streaks of soot in the gloom
Of the fog-laden air.
Passed: and if noted at all, half-unheard, half aware.
How you would miss it, that voice, if it never recurred!

THE STARLING

The starling claps his wings and stoops his head,
Scattering sound like beads from a cut thread:
He washes with the skies for morning pools;
Some drops are rolling yet upon his plumes.

THE MULBERRY FEAST

Come all you winged fellows
Where the mulberry feast is set;
Hush your tunes and whet
Your bills of yellow.
Come birds smooth and spangled,
Of olive, jet, cinnamon,
The clusters break upon,
And deftly angle
Your nimble shears among them;
These shining leaves and crisp,
Shaken so they lisp,
Summer has hung them
With beaded fruit. So many! –
Yet here's no need to vie,
Swift head and eager eye,
You'll not lose any.
Like sea-bathers plunging

In the surf and the lifted sprays,
On heat-heavy days,
Ring to their lunging
My moments: their laughter
Of clapping mirth, musical,
Sweetens the fall
Of the leaves coming after.

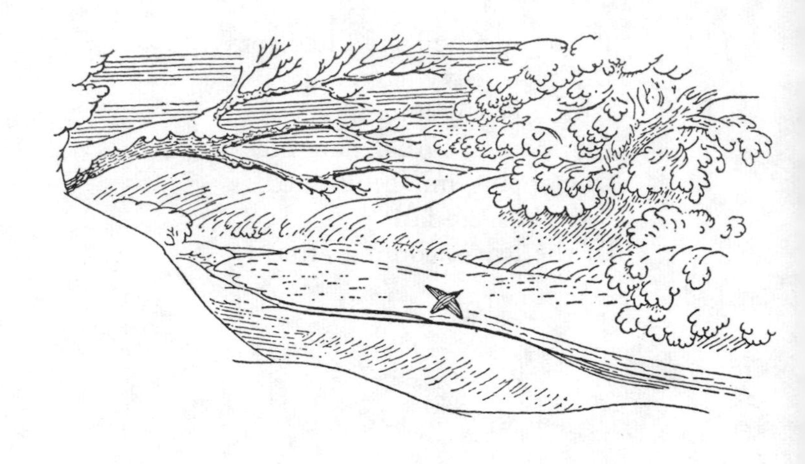

THE REDBREAST

The redbreast smoulders in the waste of snow:
His eye is large and bright, and to and fro
He draws and draws his slender threads of sound
Between the dark boughs and the freezing ground.

BIRDS IN WINTER

No last late berry, bloomed with frost,
By their sharp eyes left unespied,
Now lingers like a jewel lost
In russet falls of tangled hair.
Along the meadows combed and bare
The buffed, rain-sodden grasses, tied

In wisps by wind, and snarred with burrs,
Are poor of few or bitter seed.
The woods where beechmast diapers
The earth, and shelly overstrow
In hazel coverts, can but show
A pittance to their driving need.

Beneath the agate, smooth and dim
As perished ardour, of the sun,
With livid lip and poisonous brim
The hunger-blossom singly thrives,
And honey which the bee Death hives
Is there conserving, – food of none.

When robed with pallor are the skies,
When with unebbing and quick rage,
From heights where very silence dies,
The north wind like a breeding haste
Of flame wood-havens has laid waste,
And every green brook-harbourage,

They temper under drifted sills
The snowfall, and with mantled plume
And drooping raise their slender bills
Against the dire winds cut and thrust,
Down-dealt with every crooked gust,
Whilst over them the dry flakes fume.

And of their muster can not one
Let palled into the frosted air
One song, in memory of a sun
Veiled and enshadowed as in dream;
Not one frail tune, that such might seem
The ghost of Summer misted here!

THE JAY

Her breast is like a rose,
And her back is like a jewel;
She gives her music to our eyes,
Her voice is harsh and cruel.
Yet she warns everything that runs
From crueller men with harsher guns.

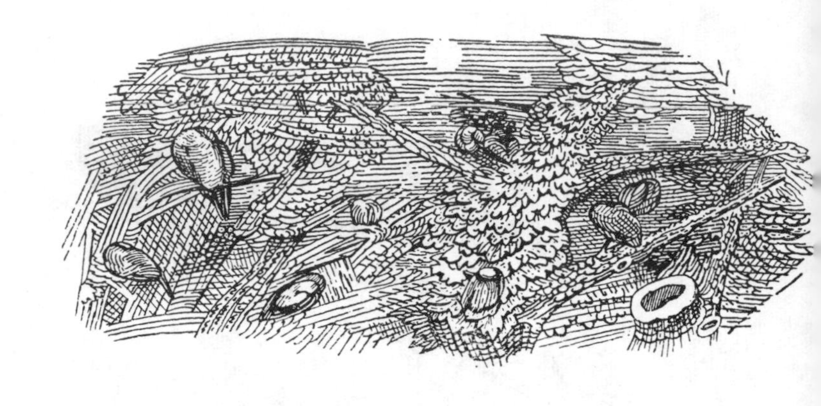

WINTER SLEEP

How long the night must seem to little birds a-cold,
High upon open boughs; in hollow ancient trees!
The ivy where they hide forbids them quite to freeze,
But shallow is their sleep, and full of miseries.

O memories of warmth and the rounded ears of gold;
The sun, and the blue air, and the wind among the sheaves
As in and out of dreams uneasily it weaves,
How must each body shrink when, waking, it perceives!

How long is winter? It is a night of years;
Each year a night; a winter's night each hour:
How weak must seem these lives, against how vast a power!
How keen the will, if these may come to flower!

Pray they may never wake, than, failing, wake in fears:
Pray they may never wake, than wake to know their need;
But, dying into fields, may sip, and cull the seed;
Sing the clear song, and fly forever freed.

THE LITTLE OWL

Sparse elder and few thorn
Bedeck the burial mound,
Where the dead keep forlorn
Their cold unhallowed ground.
They lie there quite alone,
While in the boughs wind-shorn
The westerly winds mourn;
For though the Little Owl,
Squatting on stump or stone,
Weeps like an earth-bound soul,
He is to them unknown.

He does not cry to come
To other gale-blown trees,
More calcined hills, of Spain
That was of old his home;
But, spectre-flitting, sole,
He calls, and claims in vain
The fellowship of these:
Ghosts, who know not his name!

TREE-CREEPER

Bird delicate and brief,
The Creeper, upward going,
Spirals the trunks of these
Sea-weathered, bare elm trees,
Against the veiled blue winter sky,
In wintry sunlight showing:
As if a brown, decaying leaf
Back to the branch were blowing.

THE COCK PHEASANT

Deep in November woods, burning, a sullen jewel,
Where the dark yews far over lean with their sombre hoods
Under the amber bracken lurking when winds are cruel,
    Secret and still he broods.

Or like a living ember, dwelling in ashes deep;
Like them a flake unfevered seeming to lie subdued;
But which a breath remembers, causing to wax and leap
    In a brief flame renewed.

Or like a sultan exiled forever his splendour,
Whom the close bounds of a prison strictly immure,
Forfeit the crown and the pomp, the imperial candour,
    Proud-stepping still to endure.

Look! – Where your footstep has roused in incautious approach
Flashes the gem in the crown as the glory prevails: [ing
Rushes the flame of his sound to its summit, and breaching
    Silence, as suddenly fails!

THE WOOD OWL

What music, this – high and remote,
Fleeting above the frozen earth?
Vision-translated wreaths that float
Of wood-smoke undulant blown forth!
What lovely sound! What subtle birth!
Music attenuate, tremulous, clear;
But with a high elusive mirth
Only the child-of-heart can hear –
Has ever heard: – not mortal cheer.

BARN OWL

This is the old, immortal bird,
Phantasmal through an age of night,
Whose bitter travesties of tune, once heard,
Faint ears affright.

It is his instrument to startle flight
In shrinking things afeared,
And, as he flies, silent and white and weird,
Kindles in them, who know their end has neared,
Life's last, intensest, light.

THE SWALLOW

At sunset, to the river, to refresh our eyes:
To see people walking there, happy likewise;
Where the sipping swallow slants with sickle wings,
And the swan-linked image dashes with his rings.

BIRDS, THEIR DOUBLE NATURE

Out of their shaggy eaves
Have you seen sudden swifts
Into the dazzling air
Write skiey hieroglyphs?
Or from some sullen cliff
Hanging immense and sheer
Burst with impassioned wings
The hawk inhabits there?
One moment crouched and swathed
In darkness, hidden, still;
The next, the azure scythed
With wild and vibrant quill!

And, for the lesser things
That lurk or disappear
In masses thick of leaves,
How many honeyed drifts
Lives secret and austere
Preserve, where shadows lift
And tremble like their fear?
Scarcely our eyes perceive
Or ears detect how soft,
Though ever of rest bereaved,
They flit and shrink and pass –
These seeds of silence here,
That break and flower aloft!
The lark that runs in grass;
The dunnock by the wall;
This demon have they all,
This double life they share!

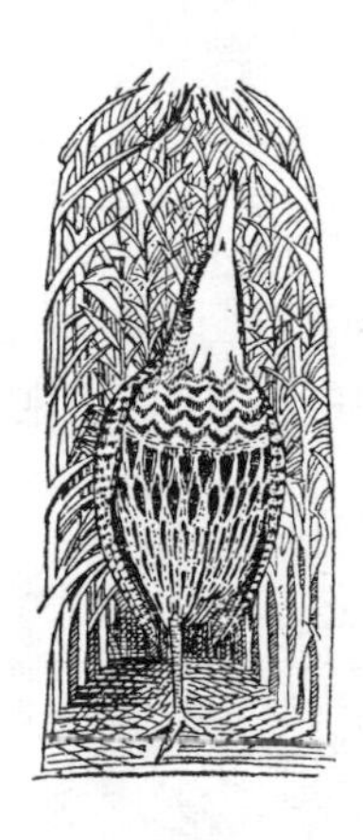

LOYALISTS

In the lulls of winter; in the trough of gales;
When earth lies bleeding, with exhausted breath;
In sudden thaws; in untumultuous pauses,
When for hidden causes
Frost no more assails:
When boughs are slowly
Of all their snow diswreathing,
And life lies lowly
And touched with death: –
There are some few small voices yet prevailing
As the air thickens; while the ice is failing.

Then the speckled song-thrush, and the greater thrush,
Birds so sober-suited,
And so long-while muted,
Sing; the robin glimmers; tits, the tufting mummers
Blue of boughs of Summer,
Break the breathing hush:
The rosy chaffinch
And the lusty hawfinch,
The blown, brown linnet, and the minniot wren,
Twitter and flute it then: –
So quick to lose the thing that yet may sear them! –
Any bright day look out, and you may hear them.

THRUSHES

Winter, and thrushes bring
Their heavenly intimations;
Singing against the wind
From leafless habitations.
How, winter-voicing birds,
How will you sing
When the leaf is on the bush
And joy in everything?
Where, for those exultations,
Would you find words
Fitter than these you fashioned –
Or is the May-loud thrush
Deeper still passioned?
And if indeed you find
Words enough, rich enough,
How will you bear their rush,
When now, through winter's rough,
Already your notes are hurled –
Speaking of Spring
As if across the world!

REDSHANKS

Now will they by the waterbrooks
Urge their wild spirits to outsight
Even their own flying, fleeting bodies,
And crying out of their flight
The triple-toned delight,
Their 'Tïew-heu!'
The happy sound we knew,

With strong smooth strokes, deliberate,
Flicker along the low wet meads
Shining and white where the tidal water
Leaves ridged where it recedes
Its froth on reeds,
Beneath skies coldly blue
As their sweet 'Tïew-heu!'

And come again, and, deftly with light feet
Running upon the mud-banks, all depart;
But on that delicate substance leave the print
Of visitation, as they leave some part
Of lonely and lost beauty on the heart
Remembering anew
Their ghostly 'Tïew-heu!'

HEDGE-SPARROW

Sober-wing; shuffle-foot;
Cringing at the laurel root;
Like a robin of the dusk –
His red flower resolved to mask;
Ever creeping, tentative,
Round the places where we live,
Wary, wearily he'll sue
For what others hold their due.
But, sly rogue, the sober task;
Air of diffidence and fear;
All away from him he flings
In the Spring; and has, in lieu,
Flight and fire and flashing wings:
Then a bird of mounting, clear
Spirit, like the changing year!

BIRDS MUST SING

Comes the time of leaves breaking,
  Birds, they must sing;
Lightly sleeping, early waking,
  Must, must sing:
However long the waiting
Until the cold's abating,
Through sudden brume and sleeting,
  Birds must sing!

Comes the time of first courting,
  Birds, they must sing;
All flirting, all disporting,
  Must, must sing:
In quarrelling and teasing,
With ardour all increasing,
At last the full heart's easing –
  Birds must sing!

Comes the time of nest-building,
  Birds, they must sing;
Straw-saving, leaf-wielding,
  Must, must sing:
And when the nest is fashioned,
On boughs above it stationed,
Elated and impassioned,
  Birds must sing!

THE WREN

It was the wren, the wren,
Whistled so shrill, and then
Whistled as shrill again.
Over the brown earth bare
It seemed to run on air,
Under the feet of men
Fearlessly so to fare;
Then paused, and with the strength of ten,
'See me!' it sang. 'I dare!'

JULY NIGHTINGALES

he nightingales are silent, and into thickets fly;
n July leaves lie perdue, from heaths and commons dry.
April's adventurers
Become the Summer's pensioners,
itting with folded wings and well content;
And, past July,
nto new worlds of beauty they'll aspire or die.

f their imperial speech no syllable now reaches;
No eager tongue beseeches;
No pause is eloquent:
The night has no remembrance
Of that, nor any semblance
ear these few notes and hesitant, occluded, faint, and low,
That we, ourselves translated,
Hear as we pass so fated,
Umbered and dull and slow,
nto new hazard breaking, when the time is so.

CORNCRAKE

And when the moon above the grass-field glowed,
Still under it his slender body flowed
Along the ground, between the quiet stems;
And still he wrought his dusky strategems,
With eloquent ventriloquy: 'Crake, Crake;
Crake, Crake.' And not a ripple showed
Upon the grasses, to betray his wake
Where all night long, mysteriously, he strode.

THE KESTREL

The kestrel, wind-possessing,
On long and lovely vanes,
Her fan-wise tail depressing,
Effortlessly remains;
Then tilts and turns and fetches round
At a new pitch above the ground.

Lightly, lightly she balances,
With small fierce face inclined
And drooped, convulsive talon, sees,
Deep in each tuft entwined,
The stirs and sudden ceasings there
Apparent through the depth of air –
The little glitterings like glass
Of shards and eyes, that wink and pass.

She drops: and busy with these things
Is hidden briefly in that grass;
Then goes, with even-beating wings.

TURTLE DOVES

Turtle doves in their green cells, high,
Light as the honeycomb,
With thrilling cadence of long soft trills
Like pulses throb in the leaf-thick hills;
That time of year they're by
Is when the Elder trees are come
Near the perfection of their bloom,
In milky pannicles.

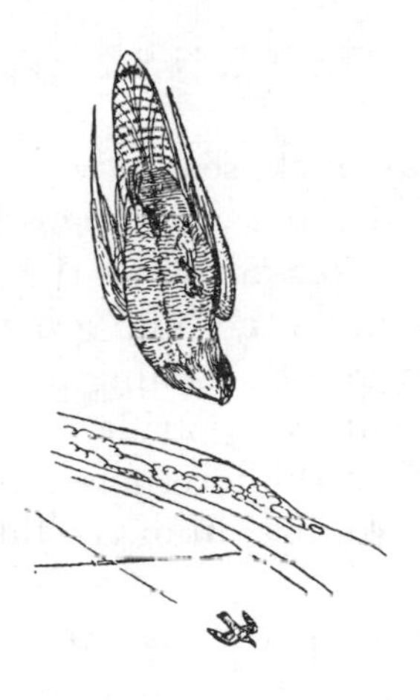

THE PEREGRINE

I saw a falcon, and a ring dove under:
She stooped; he beat his wings; and then, a wonder:
Fast as he flew to the concealing tree,
Dead, a short distance faster still flies he!
The stricken body as it hit the ground
She knit upon, before it could rebound,
And feasted on; and when she had her fill
Flew to a jut of rock, and scraped her bill.

TERNS

With sea-wrack, sea holly,
  The low dune was crowned,
Where the sea devoured the shingle,
  The shingle the high ground.
There, where the sliding pebbles
  Grated at every stride,
I walked on the foreshore
  At the coming in of the tide.

And the terns, the sea-swallows –
  Dipping they fell and rose;
No lovelier company
  Had anyone than those,
Keeping with ease their places there,
  Buoyantly at my side,
To take the small-fry shoaling
  At the coming in of the tide.

The smooth sea; the still morning;
  These, that so lightly rode
The light airs streaming shoreward –
  And me, that stiffly strode!
So white they seemed, as the waves themselves,
  Where the waves lapsed and died,
To fling in hissing fringes
  The fingers of the tide.

THE BULLFINCH

See the bright bullfinch now,
High on the apple bough,
Whose petals, open, show
Drifts of ensanguined snow!
How, while his rosy bosom
Rifles the paler blossom,
He pipes both clear and loud,
So bluff, so burly, and so proud!

Look how his plumage new
Vies with the rose in hue,
And from the thunder shade
Has cap and mantle made!
Vivid and blythe and gay,
His beauty seems to say:
'All things are happy now,
'High on the apple bough!'
While he pipes, clear and loud,
So bluff, so burly, and so proud!

A FLIGHT OF BIRDS

A magic confluence of wings,
Flowing, unfolding, like a scarf
That wind-borne rises, stretches, floats,
Then drops upon the earth.

And in that weft a thousand tongues
Are little twinkling jet-like rays,
All eloquent together raised
In one tumultuous shout.

Like thunder seems their rustling sound,
But hushed and far-off heard, or as
When driving with the tempest sings
The deluge down the sky.

Pendulous over sodden fields
They waver, like a heavy plume,
And are at last all vanished, stilled,
And gathered from our eyes.